7/22/14

Thank you Jean
for your supp[ort]

Dr. Rashara N.

DEVELOPING NEXT GENERATION LEADERS IN A DIVERSE ENVIRONMENT

LEADERSHIP DEVELOPMENT

DR. R.N. GIVHAN

authorHOUSE®

AuthorHouse™
1663 Liberty Drive
Bloomington, IN 47403
www.authorhouse.com
Phone: 1-800-839-8640

© *2014 Dr. R.N. Givhan. All rights reserved.*

No part of this book may be reproduced, stored in a retrieval system, or transmitted by any means without the written permission of the author.

Published by AuthorHouse 2/5/2014

ISBN: 978-1-4918-5758-8 (sc)
ISBN: 978-1-4918-5757-1 (e)

Library of Congress Control Number: 2014901536

Any people depicted in stock imagery provided by Thinkstock are models, and such images are being used for illustrative purposes only.
Certain stock imagery © Thinkstock.

Because of the dynamic nature of the Internet, any web addresses or links contained in this book may have changed since publication and may no longer be valid. The views expressed in this work are solely those of the author and do not necessarily reflect the views of the publisher, and the publisher hereby disclaims any responsibility for them.

Contents

Introduction vii
Chapter 1   Learning Processes 1
Chapter 2   Theorist 3
Chapter 3   Learning 7
            Definitions of Learning 7
            The History of Learning 8
Chapter 4   Learning Theories 10
            Learning Process 12
            Learning Purpose 15
Chapter 5   Teacher and Facilitator 16
            Teacher verse Facilitator 18
Chapter 6   Teacher 19
            Teaching Process 19
            Teaching Strategies 20
            Teaching Models 21
Chapter 7   Producing Effect Learning 23
            Learning in the Corporate Environment 24
Chapter 8   Adult Learning in Current Environments 27

Chapter 9   Literary Discussions..30
                 Levels within the Andragogy Practice 30
                 Training Environment 37
                 Interventionist 39
                 Introduction of Subject Material 42
                 Processing Through Subject Material 46
                 Demonstration of Learning...48

Chapter 10 Training Module..52
                 Background 52

Chapter 11 The Program 54

Supplemental Package For the Implementation
   Of this Workshop 69

References..73

Introduction

In the development of leadership for the new generation of leaders, there are many factors to consider. The leadership environment has 4 generations of individuals trying to move the corporation. The purpose of this research is to relate principles of human developmental theories and include these theories, which leadership development organizations can implement to grow the next generation of leaders. The details of these writing are an analysis, compare and contrast of educational philosophies presented by Knowles, Sticht, Bryson, and Argyris. A discussion on the strengths and limitations in adult learning and education applications shall be a part of the analysis. The primary focus is the application of models to increase the learning. In executing the models the base principle questions are required for the model, is the age group significant in the development of the model, and how does the educational level of the group impact the model shall be included. The central objective is to develop an overall application in course format for the adult working environment.

Chapter 1

LEARNING PROCESSES

There are many concepts used today to develop models for the training and broadening of the adult community. The need has developed due to changes in the population spread. Censuses have shown there are more adults in the US population than in previous years. The increase in the population has grown a need to better educate and develop the adult workforce. Various corporations have taken many avenues in the process of this development. There is an educational program in most industries, which allows the worker to further their personal growth with additional courses. The need for comprehensive training models has grown due to these programs.

The objectives are to analyze the learning theories of Knowles, Sticht, Bryson and Argyris in terms of their underlying principles about adult training: to compare and contrast the philosophies of Knowles, Sticht and Argyris from their perspectives on adult learning systems: and to discuss the strengths and limitations on present applications of adult learning processes. The theorists of this document have developed their own understanding of adult learning and the adult learner. The definition of the terms adult learner and adult learning evolve from different aspect. The adult learner is the individual taking part in the process of learning. The term adult learning is the process or model used to accomplish learning. The term describes the philosophies of the theorist.

I will start my communication by first introducing the theorist named in this document and then describing their theories. The theorists' focuses within these writings are on the works of Malcolm Knowles, Thomas Sticht, Lyman Bryson and Chris Argyris. Each developed differing approaches to the growing need for adult education. I will then expand on the objectives listed above.

Chapter 2

THEORIST

Bryson developed his theories during the early 1900's. He described the learning environment of the century. The *Adult Education* details the learning process during that time. He described much technical learning from the concepts of Thorndike's research and the application of these learning's. One of Bryson's focuses was the question of whether adult's ability to learn decline with age, beit that during the 1900's history professed that adults stopped learning by the age of 25. Bryson then documents the past methods of adult learning. He describes the use of lectures, women's club and correspondence schools etc. for the further development of adults. All of which were methods used by people order then 20. He discusses Thorndike's research stating that learning capacity did decline by 15 percent as the person reached the age of 45. He continued to do research to understand that decline. The attempt was to discover whether it was the adult's ability or the adult's desire that caused the decline. In simple terms, was the adult unable to learn or due to present industry did the desire to learn diminish? The research found that physical limitation was not the primary reason for decline. The adult's internal ability does not contributed to a decline of learning. In the process of teaching Bryson maintains a view that pedagogy methods are required. The concept that even in the higher levels of learning it is important to demonstrate these processes. The position of leader and authoritarian are required in this process. He does state though that when dealing with adults it may be necessary to remove the position of authoritarian. He advocated the maintenance of the leader position.

Knowles (2005) evolves the concept of pedagogy to develop the andragogy theory of adult learning. He focuses efforts on adult's needs and desires. The base philosophy is that of the individual and their internal purpose. He develops theories around teaching people with life experience. These theories introduce the relationships between life and learning. He further explains the significance of purpose in learning. The purpose of the learning dictates the structure, the teaching process, and strategies. He demonstrates that such modeling is very different from that of a child, which is the pedagogy process. He maintains that learning occurs when the adult needs met in the teaching process. Knowles methods are important based on the growing need for adult training course in the work environment. Knowles developed a teaching process that require specific step to creating an environment of learning. Knowles examined the effects of behavioral science and human needs to expand the process of learning.

Argyris (1982) focus is the work environment. Argyris (1993) develops his theories from a number of cases and interviews. In the examination of the individuals, involved Argyris has been able to develop a theory, which describes the process of learning or the lack thereof. He details the general approach and process of people in various problem-solving situations. He demonstrates through data, examples and role-play research actions and reactions that can be counterproductive to adults learning. The learning Argyris details is that internal evaluation, patterns, and correctness. Argyris defines the ladder of inference. The ladder of inference described is a stepping process to ineffectiveness. He specifically shows the short falls of such a process in learning. Argyris created a model that emphasizes theories in action, better defined as theories in use. Argyris argues the single –loop learning is the functioning of Model-I –Theory-In-Use. This learning for adults is the development of one's own premise and defining it as fact. By doing so there is no learning because one generally aligns the premises within their own value system. Argyris then demonstrates a model, which introduces learning system. This model structure is for the increase consciousness of the group and organization. The system allows the learning to loop back and review the data for evaluation. The method trains the individual to test it thought to be truths and develop concrete evidence to support that truth. He then improves the model b expanding the concept for Model II theory-in-use. Model II suggest attributions not founded on specific data be tested by the group for clarity. The process is useful in the event there is the introduction of fear and frustration by the group members. It provides an environment for second level learning by the group.

Sticht's approach to adult learning centered on content-based learning. Content-based learning is the process in which the information is distributed based on prior knowledge levels. The information provides the learning with an ability to connect, reflect and expand base knowledge. The learning can move the learner to a high-level of learning. The information is in the long-term memory of the learning in high-level learning. The information becomes a part of the learner's experiences. Sticht training focus was primarily in the area of learning needs. His approach has improved the learning experience for those that move to post-degree stages. In the post-degree stages, Sticht's concepts can evolve these learners to a level of conscious reflection.

After reviewing, the concepts of each theorist there are similarities in reference to the learning needs of adults. In early studies, there is more focus on the capability of the adult rather then the desire. It was found that there was and still a growing desire for adults to continue the learning process. The approach to learning changed drastically in the 60's and 70's. The pedagogy formats worked well in environments, where the student's educational level was in the remedial stages. Yet, with the growing levels of education, the teacher as the authoritarian format was not effective for many adult learning environments. Each theorist's was able to develop meaningful processes to improve the learning of adults.

By understanding these processes, Sticht was able to define content-based learning approach. This approach answered the need in the military environment. Generally, the military environment was composed of many levels of education. This process allowed the training environment to focus and deliver information as needed. The information delivery was at the level the learner required.

Knowles (2005) development of the andragogy, which contained elements of Bryson's approach, captured the need for independence and ownership by the adult learner. Knowles (2005) determined adults could learn through discussions and forums guided by facilitator or teacher. Knowles realized that this approach could be successful even in environments where the educational levels may have been remedial. Knowles would use the concepts of Sticht. Knowles (2005) developed a learning process. Knowles (2005) incorporated in the learning process the content-based approach is used to establish certain levels of control. The learning process provided the learner with elements of a good learning environment.

Argyris (1993) evolved the learning process even more. Argyris' development of theories such as Model-in-Use allows the facilitator to place boundaries around learning moments and error detection. By applying, the learning process of Knowles (2005), and applying the looping and testing of information the learner is learning. The next step would be to apply action from the learning that has taken place. When results are actions, there is an acknowledgement of learning.

Each theorist tending to build on the others detailing of how adult learning is should be modeled. Each driving to the characteristic of the adult psychological needs, all evolving from different industrial environment needs. As technology expands the learning model has to expand with it.

Chapter 3

LEARNING

DEFINITIONS OF LEARNING

Webster defines learning as the act or experience of one that learns, which aligns with the concepts defined by the fore mentioned theorist. Learning is defines by each theorist to introduce their independent views of learning. Most did not view learning as a process, yet as an independent act of the individual.

In the exploration of learning theories, Knowles (2005) determined that learning occurred when there was a change in behavior, knowledge level, skills and attitude. In Knowles' body of work, he references more the process of higher learning. Knowles stated that other theorist defined learning in different concepts such as growth, fulfillment of potential or the development of competencies. Each term refers to some type of visible result from the process of learning. Knowles (2005) highlights that fact many in the study of humanistic psychology define learning in cognitive terms. Humanistic psychologist included elements such as personal involvement, self-initiation, pervasiveness; evaluation by the learner, its essence is meaning, and self-actualization. Knowles (2005) also documents the perspectives of learning domains evaluated by educational psychologist. Knowles (2005) demonstrated this is a single process with various steps. One-step being verbal information, where the context of the information should be organized and specific to the individuals involved in the learning. Knowles (2005) summarized learning as a process of gaining knowledge, as well as expertise.

Where Bryson (1936) defined learning as a necessary process of life. He stated that as long as you live you would learn. By viewing learning from this perspective, there is no discussion of change. Change maybe expected in the process of life, yet there is no structure to evaluate that change.

Argyris (1993) took a slightly different approach to the process of learning. In the implementation of the Argyris (1993) concepts of Models-in-use and discussion, learning occurs when an error is detected and the error is corrected. Therefore, in the process of the course, the students have the opportunity to detect errors in the information provided. Once an error has been detected the exposure to correcting the error is the considered the act of learning. This process embraces the concept of change and evolving from that change. This is very similar to Knowles view, due to the fact, that the result may develop a change in behavior, knowledge level, or attitude.

Webster's view of learning described as an act or experience aligns to the process of change. The acquiring of knowledge is an act. We cannot determine the result of this acquisition process. Action is the result of whether there is a change in behavior or skills. In Argyris's theory of Model-in-use learning, the action taken is the correction of an error.

THE HISTORY OF LEARNING

The theorist reviewed to understand the history of learning was Bryson (1936). Knowles (2005) discussed some portion of the documented history, yet his information was documented references. Bryson spoke to the various formats of learning that took place in the early 20th century. Bryson compare the American system to that of other nations. He described their progress and short falls. Bryson describes methods such as lyceums, women's club and correspondent schools. During this time, these were the major forums used to educate people. It is interesting to note that during this time education was limited to certain individuals. The industrial environment and community determined the need for education. Many people during this time were farmers and the educational environment was the responsibility of the core family structure. Certain types of education had little to no value. The World War changed the need for training and adult education. The need to educate immigrants grew during this time also. Many other factors contributed to the need for teaching and educational institutions in America. Developing education processes made America one of the most powerful nations in the world. Bryson's book noted that 1926 was the turning point of the educational revolution.

Chapter 4

LEARNING THEORIES

Knowles exploration of learning theories determined that there are two major families of learning theories. The families of theories are behaviorist/connectionist and cognitive/gestalt. These families align to the sets defined by theorist Taba and Gage. The process analysis developed elemental and holistic models for learning theories. Each of these models evolved from different theorist such as Thorndike, Watson, and Dewey.

In the elemental model the concepts of stimulus and responses were developed. The action of developing a behavior based on actions of the facilitator provided a basis for understanding the mental processing of humans. The study gave foundational concepts for behavioral systems. Knowles define the elemental model, as the universe as a machine composed of discrete pieces operating in a spatio-temporal field, which is reactive and adaptive model of man.

The holist model bases its focus more on theories developed by Dewey. This movement gave birth to the concepts of functionalism. This theory rejected ideas that learning is based on a response from some stimuli. They focused this model on the concepts that a sequence of responses based on varying stimuli was the learning process. All of which evolved human behavior studies and fields of knowledge. From Knowles perspective holistic models are the as a unitary, interactive, developing organism, which is active and adaptive.

In either process, Bryson (1936) aligned himself with both lines of thought. Bryson (1936) discusses deeply the need during 1930's for more functionalistic views of learning. Bryson continues to define various functions of learning during that time. Functions meaning overall reasons for learning, such as remedial, occupational and liberal, they are all functions of learning in this millennium. Each function provides the adult with some form of self-development and self-direction. The purpose of remedial learning was to move the adult to a minimal level of education for the better citizenship. Better citizenship was the underline reason for occupational and liberal as well. Occupational applied in a different capacity. The liberal learner learned to expand their base knowledge and understanding of the world. We face this same issue today with the high level of illiteracy, the constant change of industry standards and the need to understand beyond our borders.

Bryson (1936) makes a statement that adults continue their learning because they have elected to do so. There can be forcing factors that contribute to that decision such as economic needs. These forces have great effect on what Bryson deems the learning power of an individual. In this, adults have excreted a level of control over their learning process, where as younger student i.e. children tend not to have that control. Bryson (1936) makes a great point in that once adults reach the age of 30 they are at their highest level of learning. There is no need to continue for the sake of learning or continued development. This is where the role of the educator is profound. The educator must relate to the adult learner that there is a need. The educator's role is the key in the learning environment to convey that important process.

Bryson (1936) details that due the experience level of adult learners there is a great need for the educator to help the student develop extend methods of thinking and processing. A system without biases is important to maintain. The educator's responsibility to the learner is to guide them in the process of expedition, which can lead to skepticism. Investigation happens by inferring doubt to the logic of the learner. Various paths to the solution develop by the learner. The process may call for data findings and/or a review of cultural systems which the learner has developed their thinking. This allows the learner to be more active and exploratory.

Argyris' work focused more on moving the individual from an element process to a more holistic process in learning. In the Models-in-Use I, there is a very deep connection to relying on perceived premises that may have not truth. The actions from the learner are reactive to the information. There is an elemental process of collecting data, storing and reviewing data with second level inference. This moves the individual to react to information stimuli. The validity of that data is not questioned in this process. With the development of the Model-in-Use II, the need remove the levels of inference are required. The Model-in-Use II allows the individual to become active in the learning process by not responding to the information but expand the information. This is more holistic in process because there are more than one stimulus and many responses. The process allow the learning the opportunity to learner from detected errors in the data.

The implementation of either process is valid based on you student body. When adults are in a primary learning environment then maybe the elements concepts are appropriate. The teacher/facilitator should understand the audience. Every day development of new theories occurs. The changing environment in which we leave requires such action. The move of technology and the need for evolution are major contributors to this process. In order to maintain educational advantages and world performance this area of study has to grow.

LEARNING PROCESS

The process of learning though viewed differently based on ones area of knowledge is the logical steps to achieve a specific objective. In developing the process, factors considered were age, need and environment. Knowles and Argyris developed distinct processes for conveying information to adult learners. Each process provided the adult with clear solutions to the needs of adults in the learning arena. Bryson's approach seemed to be the foundation for both Knowles and Argyris.

In Bryson's, Adult Learning, body of work, he describes methods used to teach adults. He discusses the following lecture, discussion, forums, radio, laboratory and studio work, correspondence and self-directed study. During this time, all avenues were being used to education the American people. The face-to-face processes were thought to provide the student greater opportunity for learning. Bryson notes that the lecture format was becoming unpopular and losing its appeal. Very few adults wanted to go to classrooms and sit for hours with someone lecturing to them. The discussion format was more popular based on the prior educational level of the student. The discussion environment gave the student a platform to provide and receive information. This expanded the experience of the adult, which resulted in greater learning. Forums where structure on larger topics and generally was a method used to introduce ideas. Rarely was the environment open to valuable discussion or review. To a certain degree, the radio process was very similar to that of forums. There were methods used to convey new ideas and provide information.

The laboratory and studio work aligned with a holistic view of learning. The laboratory allowed the students to be hands on with the process. It gave the student immediate information in the process of learning. The approaches of correspondence course and self-directed study were very new during the 1930's. Yet, they moved adult learning to the next level of independent learning and independent growth. These formats made the adult more responsible for their own completion and evolution.

Knowles development in andragogy embraced the psychological needs of the adult. Bryson wanted to move adults to that position, yet Knowles believed most started in that position. Knowles embraced the fact that adults had established thought processes and information. Information gathered through life experiences. This being the foundation, from which adults worked, developed a requirement to understand these foundations. Knowles also took into account Maslow's hierarchy of needs and the affect these had on adults learning. Most would not consider the environment of learning as being an item of importance. Based on human psychology it is. Knowles then developed a strategic view of learning based on the type of learner you may have. There are three categories adults align to 1) goal-oriented, 2) activity-oriented, or 3) learner-oriented, each provide a strategic approach for the facilitator. The facilitator can then review type of learning usage, Knowles describes theorist Gagne's list of types of learning. Here is a list of those types: signal, stimulus-response, chaining, verbal association, multiple discrimination, concept, principle, and problem solving. The facilitator's strategy is composed of the learner's purpose and the type of learning that needs to take place.

Argyris' approach defined learning in the detection of errors. He discussed the method of providing an environment where individuals can inquire, confront and make vulnerable people in the learning. Argyris' allows people to communicate and evolve. He looks to limit counterproductive behavior that would inhibit learning. Argyris' process is structure in the following way; discovery, invention, production and evaluation and generalization. These processes should be implemented using double loop learning procedures. For double looped, learning the facilitator should develop an environment where learning from the data can take place on the first and second rungs of inference. That is the data provided is observable, culturally acceptable, and publicly testable. In the process, the facilitator should uncover any inconsistencies or data that is not observable. Testing data, testing defensive routines and empathizing with emotionally responses assist in double-looped learning.

By implementing specific methods of Bryson, with strategies of Knowles and Argyris' concepts of double-looped learning, we can produce a systematic facilitated engagement for learners to expand their experiences.

LEARNING PURPOSE

Unlike children of today where education is part of development, adults can select to continue the process if desired. Today statistics show that the US has an extremely high high-school dropout rate. We rank twenty-seventh in the world when it comes to education. Of the US population, approximately thirty-five percent of the population has higher-level degrees. In the new presidential administration, there is a goal to increase the number of degreed Americans and to eliminate the desire for children to drop out of high school.

Adults taking classes today are goal-oriented, activity-oriented, and learner-oriented. The goal-oriented learner is in the educational process to achieve a specific objective. This objective applies to the person's employment. The activity-oriented learner is a course-taker. This means that generally there is no real objective in the learning. Most activity-oriented learners have no connection to any life situation that has caused them to take on this learning. The learner-oriented person is there for the knowledge. They are there to acquire more information. Learning for this person has always been a way of life.

In a strategic approach for adult learning, it is important to get the adult learner committed to the process of learning. By doing this, the facilitator is sure to evolve any of the types of learners. This even aids the facilitator in moving the learner to a self-directed process in the learning. This commitment produces the purpose in the mind of the learner.

Chapter 5

TEACHER AND FACILITATOR

In the environment of adult education, the terms of teacher and facilitator have been interchanged yet they are very different roles. Bryson describes the teacher as having certain responsibilities' to the student. One major responsibility is to make the subject matter enticing enough to promote a form of self-education. Others include developing an alertness and reasonable amount of skepticism. In this process, the teacher should always remain leader such that the guidance required for the adult learner is always present. In the position of leader there is a caution stated in the implementation of information. This caution focuses us around implementing or implanting the teacher's opinions without filters. By being aware of this, the teacher can rationally encourage the students to develop systematic themes of their own. In any event, the adult learner engages in the process of learning for different reason. The reason for the adult learner can be one of the learning purposes. The teacher has to aware of the foundation of the adult learner and their social need. The teacher needs to expand the internal level of the adult regardless what the subject matter. This can involve the teacher can changing to that of an instructor.

Knowles determines based on Rogers (1969) that teaching is instructing. Rogers stated that he would prefer to impart knowledge rather than teach. Knowles highlights that the actions of imparting knowledge is facilitation. Knowles states that the role of the teacher is facilitator. The necessary attribute of the teacher is ability to move the teacher-student relationship to a more personal relationship. Knowles states that a facilitator has three very important qualities. The attitude of the facilitator should be one of genuineness, trust and respect, and empathic understanding. The position of facilitator requires one to be a listener. The facilitator has to listen beyond the spoken word.

Argyris takes a slightly different path to the role of teacher. Argyris labels the position as interventionist. In this role, the person responds in an empathic fashion as well as critical. Critical in the sense that questions are introduces to increase the learning process and engage all parties. The interventionist provides test for data and assisting the learner in systematically reviewing their internal premises. The interventionist must have the same attitudinal approach as that of a facilitator to guide the error detection.

Adult learning in the new millennium is very different due to the vast amount of access to information. Many higher-level institutions focus more on having facilitators rather than teachers. The systems of today call for classrooms to have more flexibility in the process of learning. The facilitator has the ability to set the mood of the course. The facilitator aids the class in reaching an internal purpose for being in the class. The facilitator then opens the class to grow the aspirations of the class in the implementation of the data provided. The facilitator is a flexible resource for the course and can assist the student in getting additional resources if needed. As a leader, the facilitator is aware of their limitations and levels of risk they are willing to take. The facilitator has the ability to empathize and contain emotionalism experienced by the students. The facilitator is one of openness and void of basis.

TEACHER VERSE FACILITATOR

Adult education in the twenty-first century seems to require more of a facilitator. Human behaviorists denote the process for adult learners to be very different from that of children. Because the personal relationship needs are vastly different and the internal experiences of the adult are border the position of teacher should be more of facilitation. The adult learner has gather data in the years of living and work. To instruct, teach someone with such large amounts of internal data can be difficult. Adults align the information presented with the information and experience stored. To attempt to teach with the unknown data unrevealed can place the course in jeopardy. Without flexibility and openness to data outside of the text, the teacher can be view as incompetent and incapable of instructing.

Facilitators and even interventionist can provide an environment for adult students to learn. The openness and communication cycles that need to happen should be a skill of the individual. Understanding your role as a facilitator and the social need of the students can supply the class with freedoms to explore and connect data for continued growth beyond the structured classroom.

Chapter 6

TEACHER

TEACHING PROCESS

Adult learners are more complicated in structured course due to their external experiences. Therefore, the facilitator has to understand some preliminary view of the group taking the course. Both Knowles and Argyris define detail processes for developing an adult class. Bryson's provides various methods based on the function of the class. The development of a process to assist in the conveying of information is an elegant approach. It also shows that there is logic and a systematic thought implemented in the delivery. What Knowles found, based on humanistic psychology, adults have certain needs. Knowles developed a systematic process to assist the facilitator in meeting those needs. The desires of the student for intellectual growth are met, while the information distribution is complete. Argyris developed models for learning rather than processes. Yet, Argyris' body of work gives readers the opportunity to develop their own processes. This development depends solely on the group one is the interventionist.

Knowles' (2005) process is as follows:

- Preparing the Leaner – Provide information, prepare for participation, develop realistic expectations

- Climate – Relaxed, trusting, mutually respectful, collaborative, supportive, authenticity, humanness
- Planning – Mechanism for mutual planning by learners and facilitator
- Diagnosis of Needs – Mutual Assessment
- Setting Objectives – Mutual Assessment
- Designing Learning Plans – Sequence by readiness, Problems unit
- Learning Activities – Experiential techniques (inquiry)
- Evaluation – Mutual measurement of program, mutual re-diagnosis of needs

Each bullet provides the facilitator with a logical path for execution of a learning plan. This method bases is process learning rather than content. In this format, the adult learner is an active part of the planning and success of the course. Throughout the steps, the adult learner and the facilitator are building a personal relationship and mutual commitment to the course. Within each bullet, the implementations of Bryson techniques are useful. The practice of Bryson's methods of discussion expands learning.

TEACHING STRATEGIES

The accomplishment of strategic implementation takes place when the facilitator studies the class participants and deeply understands the needs of the students. In Sticht's body of work, the process of understanding the audience and the delivery needed was a success. Sticht analyzed the generally student characteristics and met the need.

Following his lead in content delivery, integrated with Knowles process for mutual assessments can provide the facilitator with attainable tactical goals. In developing a strategy the facilitator has complete an overall assessment of student, subject, cultural environment and historical methodologies. Strategies help in understanding the flow of the course and allow the facilitator to align the course purpose with the course objectives. Overall, the strategy is vetting of the plan to meet the needs of the adult learner.

TEACHING MODELS

In modeling a concept, theorist provides a communication tool for the public. Models give a framework for how various action implementations. Earlier I referred to Knowles process as being a model. The process model is developed for the andragogy theory. For the pedagogical process is a content model, more akin to Stich's content-based theory.

Argyris developed models for the corporate environment. Argyris based his theory on behavior analysis of adults in the working environment. The models define logical steps adults take in the communication. The analysis documents the pre-judgments and review adults complete in various cultural environments.

Argyris starts with a ladder concept in how adults process data and development conclusions. The first rung of the ladder is inference. This is where adults take in data and developed premises based on that data. This may evolve to a second rung in the ladder. The second rung is also inference because the data is not tested for truth. Rather the information is thought to be truthful. The process implemented controls the environment of people involved in communication. The standard process moves people in to defensive routines of communication. A defensive routine is a process where there is unilateral control over the information provided. There is no mechanism to test the validity of the data provided. The desired model to use allows the participants double –loop learning and limits defensive routines. The Model-In-Use II concept removes unilateral control of information. It opens the door to communicate freely and with fear. The model allows participants the avenue and opportunity to validate the data provided. The validation of the data is the system used to promote double-loop learning. This removes the placement of participant contribution based only on inference. The detection of error onus information within the looping allows growth, respect and perspective to develop in the system. The defense mechanisms removal allows for committed openness.

Knowles example of model refers to a Whole-Part-Whole Learner Model in adult training. The first part of the model requires the organizer be fully involved in the development of materials and environment. This is the "first whole". This structure produces an integrated openness between the facilitator and the learners. In the process, the facilitator must find an approach, which moves the class to schemata alignment. The learning is better facilitated when the adults realizes a change in their cognitive fields and a change in their personal motivation and internal needs.

The facilitator can then segment the learning. The segmentation allows the learner to connect the information to internal data. Earlier the statement was made that adults learn through connectism and reflection. The reflection and connections take place from their life experiences and previous education. The more connections made by the facilitator the better chance there will be change in the adult's internal data. This is the second whole of the Whole-Part-Whole Learner Model. The facilitator is able to expand the information data of the learner.

The integration of Argyris process "testing the data" and connectism approach from Knowles can be a power model to implement. The incorporation of both processes moves the student to a more open and honest environment. It builds the relationship such that the facilitator can increase the number of connects possible for the information session. This aids the facilitator produce even more effective learning.

Chapter 7

PRODUCING EFFECT LEARNING

Effective learning is the overall objective. In any process, the facilitator wants to assure that students in the class, workshop, etc. walk out of the environment learning new skills or information. In many structured classes, teachers test for the retention of data. In most corporate training very little testing, takes place. Consistent behavior modifications show corporate training results. Depending on the structure of the class, use either method.

Argyris writes effective methods to use in corporate training for employees. He describes methods to reduce defensive responses and increase openness. In many situations, there is a need to allow people an environment to communicate freely. The teaching experience focuses the interventorist to provide an opportunity to question and understand the data communicated. Model-in-Use-I moves the person through a single loop of learning and can get the learner frozen in the process. When the learner is stuck in a loop of unlearning, the interventorist can break that by introducing test of the data discussed. By intervening in the data, the interventorist can move the learners to Model-in-Use II process. Defensiveness can also hold the learners to Model I, yet the method discussed in testing the data can move the learners to the next stage.

The facilitation of data is also a method for moving people to double-looped learning. In the process of facilitating data, the interventorist is responsible for the collection and distributing the data. It assists the interventorist in controlling the discussion and enhances the learning. The process of exposing incorrect or inconsistent data can aid the interventorist in providing avenues for discussion. The learning occurs when the boundaries, fear, and misunderstanding are minimized. In all the need to maintain, an open, respectful, and honest environment improves the learning.

An additional characteristic of the interventorist is emotional intelligence. The level of emotional response can affect the learning environment. The interventionist/facilitator must be aware of the emotional reactions to presented data. By being aware of the various levels with people, the interventorist can build a deeper more impactful relationship to the learner.

The segmenting approach introduced by Knowles along with the actions of the interventorist is a model of effective learning and building communication.

LEARNING IN THE CORPORATE ENVIRONMENT

Corporations have a unique atmosphere. The atmosphere is one where people are generally well educated and have many life experiences. This requires a special approach to training and learning. Due to the level of understand of these individuals and their internal purpose for learning the training model has build relationships. The corporate environment is one of the more difficult arenas to institute processes for learning.

The corporate environment demands the facilitator has specific attributes. The facilitator has to demonstrate certain characteristics of one who is well prepared. The facilitator must understand their internal fear and respond. The facilitator must show that they have credibility. One way to accomplish this is by having an attitude of an expert. A method for building relationships can be to listen and explore personal experiences from the learners. The facilitator must know how to acknowledge a difficult learner without encouraging the behavior. The facilitator must be aware of a learner's participation. In understanding these attributes, the facilitator can adjust timing, if necessary and instructions. Questions and feedback is always appropriate in the forward movement of a class.

The approach necessary for the corporate environment should provide the learners with tangible opportunities to grow. The facilitator's review of the class body and information must align. The United States is in a very delicate position. We have the pressure to be world leaders and no completed group to accomplish it. We are in a state of training and re-training. To be competitive in the world markets new demands are on our schooling system. The need to develop more engineers and health care people is necessary. The process of teaching these groups requires detail and expertise. The facilitator's modeling and communication skill are keys for success.

Corporate training courses start in business school. These course need to also start in other schools. The need for such training in the engineering schools and medical schools continues to grow. We as a society work to meet the need, yet we are failing. An example of our failure is affirmative action training. In some corporations, the process and models are working, yet there are large numbers of corporations that have the courses. These corporations are still having EEO problems.

Corporate training requires people with in-depth understanding of the cognitive changes that need to occur and the internal desires of the learner. The need to model systems using this approach of cognitive requirements develops every day. The interesting part of this initiative is our educational statistics. We are far below average in adult development. The large number of high school drop-outs and limited education of the majority causes issues in the adult training arena. Many of these people are in the corporate environment. Many facilitators have entered the field without understanding the needs. This causes a backlash because many are using a pedagogy approach, due to the educational levels. As stated, the pedagogy approach has little consideration for the experience of the adult in the training. Due to these gaps in understanding, many training course ineffective outputs move the Human Resource department's dismal states.

Corporate training occurs at all levels. The training needs to apply to the adult group taking the course. This may require various versions of training. In the end, the people taking the courses get encouragement to continue learning and the corporate work environment improves.

There is evidence that cognitive development from certain level of inference improves the learning ability of adults. This Breadth essay has summarized and synthesized theories drawn from Knowles, Bryson, Argyris, and Stitch demonstrating that adult learning processes are vastly different in human development. In addition, similar methods in adult facilitating and adult teaching process development analyzing took place. Using the theoretical frameworks, a training process for corporate learners was modeled. The implementation of models and process is a different approach useful in developing content. The modeling concept goes beyond providing information.

The next few chapters attempt to demonstrate the strategic implementation of both educational theories. The pedagogy and the andragogy process implementation in university and corporate settings. Discovery brought forth that many of these settings conveyed information, yet rarely was there any change in cognitive process. The adult learner's evolution and motivation to learn more presented limitations. I believe with the aforementioned theorist processes, the facilitator/interventionist/teacher would provide the learner with a learning environment.

Chapter 8

ADULT LEARNING IN CURRENT ENVIRONMENTS

Current universities use Knowles and Sticht as their primary models for teaching adults. This book discusses an analysis of adult educational models and teaching methods in relationship to standard education purists and executive training systems. I will also compare and contrast how adult learning philosophies contribute to the development of present executive training models. The final discussion compares the affects of adult learning developments on a growing and diverse workforce. A review of these methods was completed to provide discussion of extending the current models for corporations of today.

The adult models used followed Knowles concept of anadargogy. The articles do not detail the exact process used in adult courses. Most documented that Knowles' learning process is a necessary structure to begin with. The application of the Whole-Part-Whole model was not described in any of the articles. It was clear though that the basic method used in teaching adults was the pedagogy. A particular business school article described the use of andragogy model in order to expand the process of information sharing. The pedagogy model was the process used in both remedial teaching and elderly environments. The pedagogy methods of discussion groups and lecture processes in adult settings structured many courses discussed in the articles. The methods of documentation provided the students with course data etc.. This approach is more applicable to teaching children, yet it is common practice.

Today's corporate environment offers additional education to their employees as describes in the articles. This is deemed a perk of the company. Once young college students enter the work environment they are returning to graduate school earlier rather than later. This sets a perfect environment for continuing education at the younger ages. This allows graduate schools to maintain their pedagogy teaching process. The student's have very little experience or information to compare the data provided. For the most part, there really is no need to change the structures for those courses. This process demonstrated that in order to developed external communication skills in the young workers there is a need to implement more of Knowles andragogy processes.

There are very few training models structured to use Argyris' process. There has been very little practice of the application in the university environment. A general practice is to use the model in the corporate environment. The article basis for further analysis of the Model I and Model II implementation exist in IEEE article journals and other corporate libraries. In the graduate student arena, due to the age group of the students, the pedagogy models are more commonly used. The practice of double-loop learning is difficult to apply due to the experience and knowledge levels. The students have very little to infer information against at that stage.

Interestingly enough the level of diversity in graduate schools and executive arenas is not significant enough to collect measureable data. The levels of diverse students entering graduate school are minimal. As well, the number of diverse executives is less than five percent. One would expect though that the inference level in Argyris' Models exist more in a diverse group, due to behavioral and cultural differences. The hope is that data shared would not be limited. Maybe in the future there will be more opportunities to implement such a process.

Overall the each approach adds value to the individual, the use of these models demonstrate an environment of openness. The demand to be inclusive in educational circles can be a great tool for innovation and productivity in industry. By reducing developed boundaries in the application of such tools, the student can evolve their knowledge base. As stated in many arenas information is gold.

Chapter 9

LITERARY DISCUSSIONS

In reviewing, the literature associated with adult learning there are very few model structures combing theory definitions of Knowles and Argyris. Both theorists took very different approaches to adult training and learning environment. Knowles (2005) dealt with many levels of cognitive behavior in adults and developed strategies for educating all of these levels. The application of his approach removed the level of cognitive behavior Argyris examined.

LEVELS WITHIN THE ANDRAGOGY PRACTICE

As stated Knowles, development focused on the aspects of the individual such that information reception is successful. There are no additional tests for information retention or behavior review. The levels align to Gagne's eight types of learning. Depending on the approach to learning, one creates the optimal learning environment. Knowles' practical model leverages levels and attributes of the individual. Knowles' documented levels in andragogy breaks down into three layers. The first or outer level refers to understanding the goal and purpose of the learning. This goal or purpose of learning can vary based on additional factors of the group. Subject areas such as behavior change or organizational change are purposes for the learning. Some consider knowledge transfers and information sharing as formidable goals.

In this level, there are areas to focus on as part of developing the course goals and purpose. These areas are individual growth, societal growth, and institutional growth. By allowing them to be the underlined foundation of the course goals, the instructor's ability alignment of course material and structure become achievable.

Within Argyris' (1982) approach, the course definition is stated. The purpose is of learning Argyris' definition are the results of those behavioral courses. Argyris' approach had little to do with the overall structure of the course. His focus was on the process of information sharing. He demonstrated that based on this the result of true individual learning could occur. The need is for the members of the course to behavior in a manner that allows the individual to limit inference and attribution. By answering questions such as: Will the outcome actually be a change in behavior? During the sessions, are changes to the individual taking place?

To align with further development Knowles' (2005) moves to the second level of the individual. The questions of what are the individual's differences and situations. This level can include things such as education and work experience or the lack there of. A great example is generally in graduate classes, the course's enrollments are people with less than 2-3 years of work experiences. This means that in the process of the course the instructor would have to supply many of the meaningful situational information to the class. As in some cases if the class has an older student, the student may have meaningful experiences that arouse discussion, to add knowledge to the class. This level can move the course to not for filling its objectives if the instructor has not taken the individual's internal situations in to account. The student with the most experiences may demonstrate power and move the course in a different direction. In this level also, the instructor may have an additional premise of this level, the individual learning differences, the individual's situational differences, and subject matter differences define the next layer of information shared. It is important included due to defining the appropriate level and information the instructor provides to the class. An example, review the equation of a line to a group of 10-15 year engineers and relate the data in management communication course. There is not relationship. The instructor may find it impossible to apply the data appropriately for meeting the course goals. It feeds back to the outer layer for a closed loop process.

Specifically, the individual learning differences center in three areas. The instructor must be familiar with these areas are cognitive, personality and prior knowledge. Knowles (2005) uses Jonassen and Grabowski, (1993) data to describe these areas.

For the cognitive area the person's ability to understand, communication and retain information are key. Knowles (2005, p154-155) focuses on a variety of aspects of the individuals abilities.

1) General Mental ability
2) Primary Mental Ability
   - Products
   - Operations
   - Content
3) Cognitive Controls
   - Field dependence/independence
   - Field articulation
   - Cognitive tempo
   - Focal attention
   - Category width
   - Cognitive complexity/simplicity
   - Strong vs. weak automatization
4) Cognitive Styles: Information gathering
   - Visual/haptic
   - Visualizer/verbalizer
   - Leveling/sharpening
5) Cognitive Styles: Information organization
   - Serial/holist

- Conceptual style
6) Learning Styles
    - Hill's cognitive style mapping
    - Kolb's learning styles
    - Dunn and Dunn learning styles
    - Grasha-Reichman learning styles
    - Gregorc learning styles
7) Personality: Attentional and engagement styles
    - Anxiety
    - Tolerance for unrealistic expectations
    - Ambiguity tolerance
    - Frustration tolerance
8) Personality Expectancy and incentive styles
    - Locus of control
    - Introversion/extraversion
    - Achievement motivation
    - Risk taking vs. cautiousness
9) Prior knowledge
    - Prior knowledge and achievement
    - Structural knowledge

This area of individual learning differences and situational differences contribute to Argyris' approaches to individual premises and attribution. The degree to which the individual allows their personal situations affects or inhibits their learning demonstrates the individual's premises. The higher the level of inference the more difficult it is for the individual to accrue new information. This level can destroy or improve the instructor's ability to achieve the course goals. In Argyris' approach to question these premises and develop new knowledge, learning is accomplished. By using the same example of the 10-15 year engineers, the instructor can question the use of the linear equation concept as a teaching and coaching illustration. The instructor can make the information relevant in the application of the material. In reviewing all of the areas of cognitive learning, the questioning format should align to some of the topic areas that

Knowles highlighted. Each of these cognitive processes can either help or hinder Argyris' method of learning. Without considering these factors, the outcome may not develop any new learning for the individual. Argyris' method makes the instructor aware of these areas of issue, but does not attempt to assist them in removing these barriers. In double loop, developing the practice to question the inference levels and attempt to remove defenses that prohibit learning are important. By combining these approaches, i.e. the cognitive learning needs and the double loop learning the instructor moves through the relationships of information with individual learning achieved.

The final level of Knowles' (2005, p149) model is andragogy practice. This level focuses on core adult learning concepts. At this time, there are six core principles that Knowles recommends when there is no data collected about the individuals of the course. These are as follows:

1) Learner needs to know
   - Why
   - What
   - How
2) Self-Concept of the Learner
   - Autonomous
   - Self-directing
3) Prior Experience of the Learner
   - Resource
   - Mental models
4) Readiness to Learn
   - Life related
   - Development task
5) Orientation to Learning
   - Problem centered
   - Contextual
6) Motivation to Learn
   - Intrinsic value
   - Personal Payoff

These core principles focus the instructor to developing a standard approach to any course. The instructor structures the course materials around the data listed prior to or during the course. By including the knowledge of the additional top layers the instructor goals and objectives are more obtainable.

Within the Argyris approach, some of the above topic areas are valuable subject matter for questions. In removing individual defenses and discovering such things as the student's motivation for learning the instructor delivers the material to meet the need of the student. By following, the standard principles even in meetings with individuals the concept of acknowledging the individual needs and attempting to remove attribution learning is achievable.

The premise is that all information produces some type of learning, yet that may not always be true if the instructor/facilitator has not taken Knowles' three level into account and apply the double loop process of Argyris as required to re-enforce information. The desire is to remove defensive barriers and develop behavior changes. The behavior changes may stem from the learning that has taken place.

Let us review this in a practical sense. First level what is the individual's purpose or goal? Second level what format do these individuals learn best are they college graduates? What is best method for conveying the information to meet their cognitive styles? Will there be anyone with prior experience? Level three structures such that I do not have the prior information about the individuals but move in the manner to close the loop of structured learning. Level three answers the same questions from a different angle. What adds value is the double loop questioning on what is the student true goal and motivation, which is one of Knowles core principles. The analysis of the core principles in the process is the action of the double loop process. This process functions in the same manner as andragogical learner analysis. To understand the needs of the student the andragogical learner analysis of the six core principles provides the instructor with data to improve learning. Asking the questions is part of this process in collecting information to determine student's premises and attributions. It assists the instructor in implementing the six core principles. This implementation produces new information and new information is new learning. New learning develops new response and new understanding. The implementation of new understanding results in new behaviors. The six core principles implanted in the Argyris looping illustration below demonstrates the relationships that exist in these principles and the double loop theory.

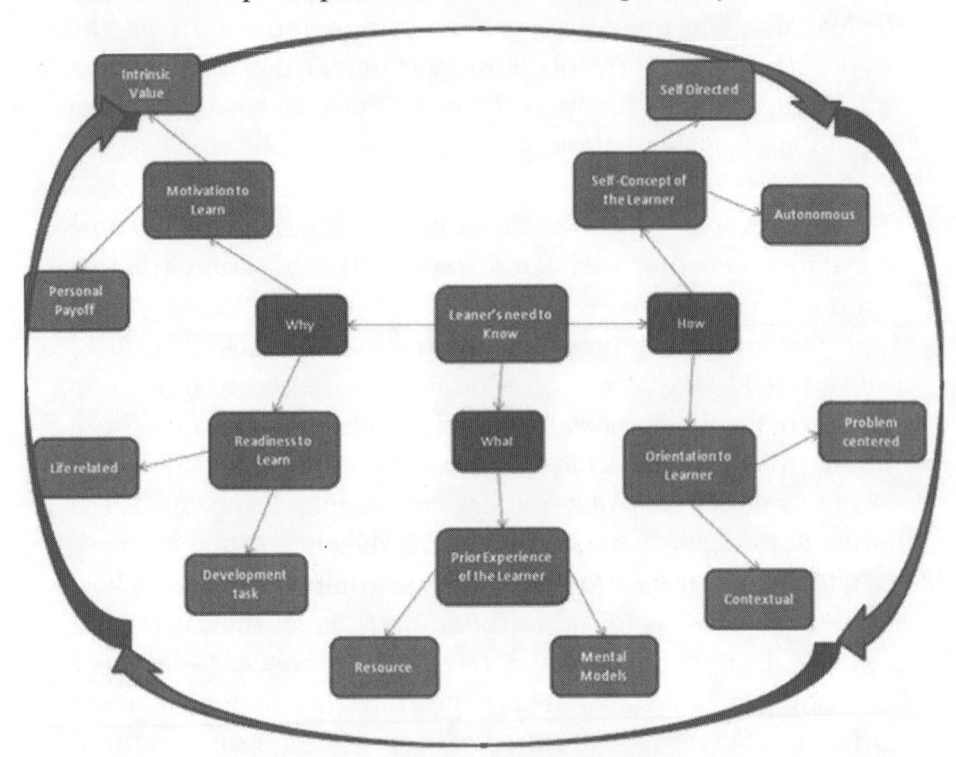

Figure 1 Knowles Six Core Principles

The double loop theory implementation broadens the instructor's knowledge in how information presentation to respond to those relationships. Depending on these factors, the instructor can test or as Knowles states it challenge the learner in their underlined premises.

The deeper the understanding of the six core principles and the application of Argyris' double loop testing, the greater opportunity for new learning by the individual in structured courses.

TRAINING ENVIRONMENT

Another area important to the successful implementation of training is the environment. The term environment's definition has two different things here. In one instance, it refers to the physical surrounding of the student. In another sense, it is the cultural background and life style of the organization. Organizations are living organism with their own inherit norms, which contribute to the functioning of the organization.

The first focus is on the culture of the environment. The term culture definition, in this process, is the person's customs and traditions. An example of this is in developing a management course with a diverse work force. Depending on the company's commitment to diversity, there may be a need to re-align the material for openness. The determination of the environment is crucial to providing a safe space for individuals to open up and become venerable. This is important in the implementation of Argyris' process because members in the course must allow individuals to communicate without fear. Having the opportunity to question the premise of individual may seem threaten to some. The purpose of the action is to understand and correct where there may be incorrect data conveyed. The environment analysis is also a part of Knowles' core principles based on the data reviewed with the student's readiness to learn and prior experience. Individuals core responds are from these primary areas. Based on the types of cultural environments they live and work in may dictate their external responses. The instructor is responsible to have some understanding of the student's cultural norms.

Even this area may develop unfounded premises by students; therefore, it is important to provide a space of openness and inquisition. This inquisition will also be a moment of learning for the students. Therefore it is important analysis both concepts of culture. As stated culture is a person's customs and tradition. The expansion of this concept includes the person's philosophy of life. Each of these definitions is contributors to an even more granular understanding of the environment.

Cultures exist in the work place. The culture of the work place develops from external influences. Meaning the workers of this environment transfer their personal belief systems on the environment. It is the responsibility of the instructor to understand the impact of such environments on the conveying and reception of information. In this instance, the environment definition is the culture the workers have produced. This environment contributes highly to the success and failure of many courses. The core principles of this environment's definition rest in the power structure with the workplace. These types of cultures are more difficult to define. They are also more difficult to prepare for in course development. The examination of such environments is imperative during the implementation of the course itself.

From another perspective cultural understanding of the individual students i.e. customs, ethnicity, and traditions are key strategic areas to review. The instructor should understand that in some cultures it might deem it impolite to question leadership. This is a hindrance to Argyris' approach beit that the process is the question statements and premises of individuals in the course. In any case, these areas within the environment need analysis to develop a strategic approach to providing, gathering, and improving data.

Knowles (2005) determined that the external or physical environment is as important to learning as the cultural environment. Knowles discussed the importance of making the area of learning astatically pleasing to the students. He describes these areas as requirements for basic animal comfort. He includes food, seating, lighting, and even acoustics of the room. The food may be either a full meal provided or refreshments provided during the sessions. The focus being by providing these you is meeting the lowest need on Maslow's hierarchy of needs chart. Suggestions from ecological psychologist state size and layout of the physical space have an affect on the quality of learning. The arrangement of seating developed and analyzed for various proximities to meet communication needs. The building lights need consideration for the training environment, as well to create an environment of openness and comfort. One addition area to take great care in is materials. The preparedness of the instructor is a crucial part. The needs for pamphlets, handouts, DVD's or CD's are part of the learning environment. The instructor's planning of materials includes the task of how data transmission takes place. The level of completeness and appearance of materials will draw or drive the students into the learning environment. The instructor must also be able to provide extra materials, such as pencil, paper, pads, and etc.., if needed for course participation.

By providing such environments, behavioral psychologists acknowledge that these components reinforce many of the desired behaviors to maintain the learning environment. With the appropriate environment studies show that student motivation and transfer of learning activities develop. As expressed by Knowles (2005), cognitive theorist determined that defined goals, clear explanations of course expectations, and open systems produce a favorable environment for learning. As well as personality theorist defined the requirement of individual respect, individual motivations, and developing an environment where feelings are just as important as ideas and skills. Knowles (2005) even describes humanistic psychologist suggestion that individuals require a thoughtful, honest, understanding, credulous, secure, and tolerant environment. The environment emphasizes cooperation and encouraging communication.

INTERVENTIONIST

All learning processes have some type of guidance or lead to assist the students in reviewing and digesting the material provided. The requirement is selecting one that can move the students to a level of learning and developing new behaviors. The requirement is to have someone defined in a role that best fits the purpose of the training. Three roles aligned to this process are teacher, facilitator, or interventionist.

The role of the teacher is the process of imparting knowledge, to instruct by precept, example, or experience. The teacher role is generally associated with the pedagogy process defined by Knowles (2005). The pedagogy process definition is the imparting of knowledge. This format is acceptable due to the age of the students in this process. The action of completing the teaching task is successful due to the student's lack of knowledge in the subject area. For general management training, most companies have determined that based on the student age group there is little to no new knowledge conveyed. The role of the teacher does not have the same meaning. In a more adult class outside of institutional processes, the teacher may use more subject examples or experiences. This process may leave the teacher open to questions of knowledge levels and expertise. In adult settings, the creditability of the teacher is important in the process of "imparting knowledge". Without the creditability, many individual defenses may appear in the students that align with their personal experiences and premises. In the teaching process, the instructional concepts require the teacher to be involved and contributing to the shaping of the student.

The next role to review is that of the facilitator. Webster states that a facilitator is one that helps to bring about an outcome by providing indirect or unobtrusive assistance, guidance, supervision. There is no imparting of knowledge but a motion of assisting people. There is no sharing of examples or experiences although that may be a function in providing the materials. As part of their responsibility, they are to make the process of receiving data/information easier. The facilitator is not the owner of the data or responsible for any learning that may need to take place. The facilitator only guides the students through the data provided. The facilitator may be a subject matter expert, yet there is no direct communication to test the validity if the information provided. The facilitator's role is to bring about productive communication. The process should not be intrusive. The facilitator may contribute to the process, yet instructionally the facilitator must remain neutral and open. The facilitator has a role to ask question. The questions open ended questions to develop communication. The facilitator only requires people to use their "Theory–In-Use", which are the person's master programs used to maintain control. The process of facilitation requires the individual to maintain control and respond unilaterally. The facilitation process recommends that facilitator control the communication. The communication is a positive process regardless to what information may need conveying. Facilitation does not require the students to test their internal belief systems. This is not to say that a facilitator cannot interrupt and move the student to a double-loop learning process. The facilitator should be aware of the opportunities to engage the student in the double-loop process. An affective facilitator can move from the teacher role to the facilitator role, while keeping the course on track. The facilitator should also understand the course layout. The facilitator should be aware of where there may be a need to impart knowledge.

The final role is that of an interventionist. Webster defines an interventionist as "to interfere with the outcome or course especially of a condition or process" or "to come in or between by way of hindrance or modification." In many of Argyris' approaches, the term interventionist defines the person introducing questions for double loop learning. The interventionist uses their insight to determine when there is a need to loop back through the data communicated. In this process, the interventionist may paraphrase the question or restate the question. The objective is to get individuals to reflect on the data communicated and analyze the answers. In relationship Webster's definition, the interventionist interferes with questioning to affect the total outcome of the information communicated. The interventionists assist in the modification of the thinking process. The interventionist role is to test the beliefs or truths of the individual. The interventionist attempts to pose no threat to anyone or even to define himself or herself as the subject matter expert. Their only role is assisting individuals be objective in receiving data and transmitting data. Their role is to move the individuals from unilateral control positions to a more vulnerable and open position. They are to assist individuals in controlling their levels of fear and embarrassment. The interventionist conveys that it is expectable to be embarrassed. Within this process, it is important to note the process of learning that takes place. By removing the defensive barriers, the reflection process and analysis of self-process contributes to personal growth. The desire is that the information produces behavioral changes. Argyris documented that the unilateral control needs of the individual may prohibit them from providing accurate data. The individual may not even speak during the session to maintain their internal control. It is the job of the interventionist to recognize that this is taking placing and interfere i.e. intervene. The interventionist is an observer to the meeting/training etc... The role of this person is very different from that of a teacher. The interventionist requirement is to maintain a learning environment. There may be a need to function in the role of a teacher but the area of expertise must me the course related. The interventionist can function as a facilitator by guiding the communication and maintaining a productive environment to continue the learning process.

INTRODUCTION OF SUBJECT MATERIAL

Earlier I spoke of Knowles (2005) third level in andragogy in practice process and detailed the six core principles of that process. To elaborate more on what I deem an important area I would like to focus on core principles two and five. This directly connects to developing a structural method for presenting the material for the training course. These areas are "Self-Concept of the Learner" and Orientation to Learning". The course material presentation affects the amount of data the learner retains. The presentation also affects the student's perceived need to change behavior. The method or process used to convey the data determines the success or failure of the course. This will also contribute to structuring needed in double loop learning.

In reviewing principle two "Self-Concept of Learning", the primary areas understood are autonomous and self directed. Initially, these areas seem similar in definition yet, based on Knowles perspective one is slightly different from the other. Adults being self-directed states that there is a self-motivation and owner ship to learning or accomplishing the task. In Knowles definition of autonomy, he suggests that it means taking control of the goals and purpose of learning. The individual assumes ownership of the learning, which also speaks to the motivation of the individual. The requirement to clarify these concepts lies in the level of commitment and motivation of the student. The two principles are driver to instructional approaches and techniques.

Self-directed suggests that the person's cognitive learning ability and style is different from one that chooses an autonomous process. The model of a self-directed person is one that takes it upon him or herself to read and reach the materials according to Knowles (2005). This process seems to translate into the individual's level of intelligence and information reception. The instructor's awareness of individual's level of self-directedness demonstrates the need for various types of communication. For example in a corporate environment the assumption, maybe that most people in the training are college educated. That is not always true. Many individuals without a higher-level education may have a high capacity to learn and understand the materials, they maybe self-directed. This moves us back to the individual's motivation. Generally, a person deemed to be self-directed is highly motivated to learn the material. In that motivation, they are eager to understand present behaviors and modify their own. The level of ownership and accountability are generally higher. The student makes internal changes as they see fit. Every facilitator wants a group of highly self-motivated people. The relationship to Argyris theory of double loop learning is the concept of processing the information for self-truths. Most self-directed learners are in questioning and reflecting modes. Their internal purposes require them to evaluate present procedures and analysis perspective changes that may be required. The self-directed learner may require little engagement from the facilitator or they may request engagement from the facilitator. The request for engagement is an indicator of awareness. This internal awareness relates to individual's level of accountability. The information processing may not align to internal perceptions.

The introduction of information for this type of individual may be at higher levels then generally, required. In dealing with self-directed students, the need for class engagement as a facilitator is limited. The role interventionist seems more appropriate. A detailed and strategic method for presenting materials is considerations in communicating with self-directed individuals.

The second area is autonomy. An autonomous learner may not go out and get the books and read for him or herself but take careful consideration in learning approaches. The autonomous learner, yet still a self-directed individual may chose to take a course to learn the material. Are they less self-directed? Knowles suggests no. He suggests that their method for self-directedness is different, but their commitment to learning is the same. He suggests the level of ownership is the same. I slightly disagree with this over arching concept. I would state that as long as the individual's level of motivation is the same then their ownership and commitment are the same. There are many cases of people selecting a structured process to increase learning but their individual commitment to the process may lag. Therefore, I would assert that the approach to conveying material should align to the needs of individuals with varying learning styles, cognitive abilities and cognitive styles. Understanding the learning level of the individual, as to whether they required a demonstrative process with direct feedback, instructional with moderate feedback, communicative with discussion, or an independent process with intervention where necessary is essential. Each level may cause a direct impact to the motivation of the individual. For example if the information is too, demonstrative the student may become less interested. As a result, they are less commitment to the course functions such as discussions. Yet, they were acting in an autonomous i.e. self-directed fashion in selecting the course.

In this process, the instructor should build a bridge to Argyris process of double loop learning. By building connective actions into the course to enhance reflective processing learning can increase. The structural layout based on individual needs assist in placement of these connections. Understanding the individual's autonomous relationship to the process and motivation can also provide connection points.

The "Orientation to Learn" is important because this focuses on a strategic learning process. Knowles (2005) states that adults are generally, problem solving centered learners rather than subject centered. With this, he states that adults learn better, when material presented are real-life examples. He suggests using contextual framing that relates to the individuals environment. He aligns this information to David Kolb's research in experiential learning. Kolb (1984) research provides four steps to understanding the experiential process. This is in direct relationship to the process of Argyris' approach to double loop learning. The four steps are concrete experience, observations and reflections, formation of abstract concepts and generalization, and testing implications of new concepts in new situations.

Because adults are problem-solvers using Argyris' approach along with the four steps developed by Kolb, the structured introduction process moves the students into an interventionist and student format. The experiential learning cycles around problem events connects the adult experiences to the information shared by the instructor. The method allows the adult to use concrete experience within their own existence and relate them to the problem statement introduced. The instructor guides the students through the material. By intervening when required observations and reflections developed to determine parallels that may exist. The introduction allows instructor to build testing data for the premises student formulate.

In taking an initial survey of the class participants, the instructor can gage the level of communication required by the course. The introduction of the material should focus on the needs of the individuals. Identifying participant's goals and aligning them to those of the course assist in building commitment and motivation. This reasoning makes the course subject matter introduction key to development of the course. This by no means suggests that the instructor's preparation for the course should be limited. Using Knowles' principles, a reasonable structure developed prior to giving the course is available.

Therefore, in structuring the course in reviewing Knowles six core principles, a sub-tier analysis prepares the instructor for all types of individuals. The method for information distribution is considerably important. Generally, all would desire that all students be self-directed and individual learners this is not reality.

PROCESSING THROUGH SUBJECT MATERIAL

Upon completion of the introduction and information shared by the participants expose additional requirements of the course; the instructor continues to transmit data for further requirements gathering from the participants. In this process, additional key core principles provide the structure to meet the course objectives. These principles are "Readiness to Learn" and "Motivation to learn". In reviewing these cores principles, the instructor evaluates the level of intervention and guidance needed by the students. I will focus on why adults choose to learn.

The principle "Readiness to Learn" correlates to the individual's life circumstances. Previous section discussion the level of instruction the student's need based on the type of course and environment of the course. Generally, corporate course or workshops have facilitators. By knowing the system, the course evolved from the method of interaction and communication develops. The methods for processing through the material are direct or support. The direct aligns more with pedagogy systems, where support aligns with adult's andragogy methods. Through this document, I discussed teaching adults in a corporate system. Therefore, the supportive role relates to the facilitator or interventionist positions. This model recognizes that adult's life experience and situations dictate the requirements for the individual's readiness to learn. The facilitator's awareness to the needs of the individual during information processing provides a solid foundation in developing a looping cycle for learning. The facilitator analyzes the environment of information and makes changes where necessary. Argyris recognized that individual's life situation might be in direct conflict to course goals. Argyris challenges the premises created by these situations. Argyris speaks to the individual's need to be in control. Individual psychology and make up requires that we control our life situations. The instructor observes and evaluates whether the life situations are pliable to allow learning. In the support role, it is the instructor responsibility to process through information and move individuals out of their theory-in-use. The theory-in-use creation stems from the individual's life experiences. By recognizing these processes in action, the facilitator may insert questioning loops where necessary. The methods assist in testing the individual's true "Readiness to Learn". If in the process the person's circumstances prohibit the instructor for recognizing where the individual is then learning may not occur. Gather the data during the introduction, determine during processing where loops should occur such that the individuals experience learning.

The next principle is "Motivation to Learn". Motivation is a driver for people to complete various task. Motivation may be external or internal. The level of motivation contributes to the individual's commitment to learning. External motivation comes from many sources i.e family, or job related. External motivations may relate to internal motivations. An external motivator such as job requirement may allow the individual fulfillment in an internal desire for success and personal value. Internal motivations are self-gratifying processes that move individuals to be self-directed. The internal motivations effectively encourage individuals by affecting one or many aspects of their life. These aspects are quality of life, satisfaction and self-esteem. Knowles' first rule of adult learning, "adults needs to know why they need to learn something before undertaking to learn it", allows the instructor to communicate a motivator for the course. As part of processing through the material, the motivator is a consistent message throughout the course.

Our theories-in-use may prohibit individuals in pursuing internal desires. These inhibits are direct contrast to individual development. In Argyris' approach, recognition of these inhibitors and testing of their validity moves the individual to double loop learning. The realignment to concrete truths may be helpful in providing internal motivators to the students. During information processing, observations of these inhibitors allow the instructor to modify the data as needed to meet the student requirements.

These principles provide the instructor with information on how to develop themes of the course, segment data for solutions, and give the student a since of achievement during. Being supportive through the process and making modifications where needed provides a steady stream of encouragement driver.

DEMONSTRATION OF LEARNING

The final core principle to discuss is "Prior Experience of Leaner". Documents show that adults learn from previous and present experiences. The use of experiential cycles assists the instructor in recognizing the individual's mental model. The knowledge of a person's cognitive process i.e schema identifies the steps necessary to progress them through the various modes of learning. The modes of learning alignment to Argyris' Single loop learning process and double loop learning process define the building block for creating a change in behavior. The change in behavior demonstrates the restructuring process in the individual.

Knowles (2005) defines three modes of learning that can result in the development of new scheme. The modes are accretion, tuning, and restructuring. The accretion mode definition is the process of learning facts that change little of the personal scheme. When adults determine the information provided aligns to data previously received there is no change in the mental model of that person. Knowles (2005) states, "Information processing theory suggests that prior knowledge acts as a filter to learning through attentional processes." (p192) In Argyris' approach, the single loop learning definition aligns to the individual's filters-in-use. This theory defines what modes and methods require the individual to maintain the internal system norms. The process of maintaining control and eliminating fear are strong emotional filters. The instructor must be aware of these emotional filters. The filters exposure comes during data gathering by the instructor. They allow the individual to maintain premises that may not be true. The tuning mode is the gradual change to the person's scheme. To affect the individuals learning mode the double loop learning process assist in limiting or even eliminating the filters prohibiting learning. Testing the in the experiential cycle progresses the individual to the final restructuring mode. Argyris' approach also develops methods for unfreezing individuals. A frozen person is one that is unable to learn. They have made a decision that the internal belief system is true. It is in agreement with the accretion mode of learning. It is very challenging to impress upon the individual that learning exist. By unfreezing, the individual change to the mental models can change the individual's inadequate premises.

In my experience unfreezing, an individual relates to understanding their emotional state. Individuals are more incline to evaluate and reflect their mental models when they are emotionally affected. Examples of this are churches. The minister's ability to move an entire room of people centers in emotional connection and charismatic communication. The ability to recognize the emotional level of the individuals assists the instructor in formulating the course requirements. Many attempt a shock process to draw fear and cause people to change. History demonstrates that such methods work to move people to action. Yet, are not 100% accurate. The truth remains though that if the instructor has the ability to connect emotionally to the individual deeper reflection takes place.

In building environments for adults to learn, the individual's background and experiences contribute highly to the context of learning. The instructor must acknowledge them and evolve the individuals in their personal experiences. For example, generally culture premises are determined to be accurate based on stereotypes. This example demonstrates the filters developed due to people's experiences or lack thereof. The instructor desire to progress the individual in this situation may be to show a film or have a speaker from the appropriate culture. The objectives are the evolution of the individual's experiences and broaden of thought.

The challenge is to reach the individual emotionally and test their personal premises that do not align to the material shared. Constructing a process that integrates the emotional development of the individual along with the defined needs of learning requires various presentation methods. Many instructors use script to build emotional relationships. Developing communication and active listening skills, the instructor can progress the individuals to demonstrating the desired outcome. By developing these skills, the double loop process is more affective such that the instructor will communicate feels and cause the individual to reflect that mode.

Demonstration of learning requires the individual to acknowledge the new learning and act upon it. The change in mental modes will contribute to the change in behaviors. The schema of the individual also changes as the learning accumulates in memory. The restructuring of the mental defines the memory structure. Changed behavior is the demonstration. In effective courses, the demonstration takes place during the course cycle. Each time the individual reflects emotionally to the process, the memories recollection. This causes a relearning for a period until the actions become second nature to the individual. It is very similar to that of teaching "The stove is hot." Each encounter teaches the lesson.

This process teaching procedural concepts the format achieves the same out come when a meaningful comparison demonstrates the need. This may appear to be a negative format to use, yet the question for the instructor to reflect upon is, "What behavior are we attempting to change in this course?". The requirement is affect individuals such that demonstrated behavior changes exist.

In summary Knowles' principles provided a stable foundation to build effective training. By including, Argyris' methods of unfreezing, single loop learned thinking and developing double loop learning activities the instructor increases learning. The restructuring of mental models and observation of behavioral changes are achievable.

Chapter 10

TRAINING MODULE

The structure of this book is to take advantage of the analysis completed in previous chapters. The initiation of corporate leadership training is to contribute to the development of extending training. The course design is for first level leaders. The facilitator gathers information that will assist in developing a strategic approach in implementing the course. The overall purpose of the course is to develop emotional intelligence and experience connections. The facilitator should be aware of the learner's motivations and course needs.

BACKGROUND

Census data shows that there will be problems in the next five years with the number of people retiring. A large part of that number is management. There is a need to develop future leaders. The next generation is dealing with a very different work force. They will have to adapt to very different environments and workspaces. Journals containing information of the upcoming need for mangers in a global market place extreme pressure on the workforce of today. They have been countless movements to develop the area. An example is the growing field of program management. In recent years, the process certification of program mangers is a focus of the United States. Certified program manager development is now the issue. The internal principles of the manager are not analyzed attributes. The core values of the person are unreviewable characteristics.

Chapter 11

THE PROGRAM

This section is the discussion of a course providing new leadership with the ability to evaluate their internal compass and make better employee decisions. The intended audience is any first level manager in the corporate environment. Presently, there is no preliminary implementation environment. The previous chapters provide a facilitated course using a Whole-part-Whole model to teach first level managers.

The intention of this book is to relate knowledge discussed in pervious sections to build a course that develops emotional intelligence to the new manager. The theoretical frameworks suggested are those of Bryson (1936, 1938), Knowles (1966, 1984, 2005), Argyris (1923, 1982, 1993), and Stitch (1976). The following section will address preliminary work requirements for the course. The course structure itself and various tools that to use to promote learning.

Need for the Program

Every company has first level managers. In recent years, the employee base has become a more diverse working group. Every company has a central level of initiatives. These initiatives align with the companies chart, goal and core values. A core value is for example customer commitment. Generally, very few employees have a dislike or disconnection from this value. The process can be interesting when the company's core values structure is around profit items. An example is global growth.

The concept centers around the company's growth index, where products, workers and development focus on the global market. The conflict comes when the manager's value system bases is completely on United States and country, "American Made". How should the manager respond and support the program? How should the manager support people for which they are responsible?

This course walks the manager through discussion point reflect of initiative that conflict with the manager's core value system. Also covered is how the manager can resolve that issue.

Course Structure

The model used is that of Knowles (2005). He describes a learning model in Whole-Part-Whole. Then implement double loop learning discussed by Argyris (1982). It is structure to produce connections to events and situations for development.

The Whole-Part-Whole process is a template from Knowles pp 249 (2005). The course has the following sections for management training. There are seven sections to the process and the list is below:

- o   Objective/Purpose of training
- o   Illustration of good/bad performance
- o   Conceptual Model
- o   Elements of the model
- o   Techniques
- o   Practice/role playing
- o   Managerial implications discussion

This is the general model used in the curriculum structure of this training.

The basic elements of Andragogy are implemented in the complete course development. This is the time to align the learner's expectation with the facilitator's expectation.

Preparing Learners

Many companies use employee surveys to determine the level and need for management. In review of the results, the facilitator can suggest various readings to set the environment. In developing this course I have recommend the learners read and review "The 21 Laws of Leadership", John Maxwell, 1998. The need is to set the learner's mind in what makes a good leader. The information allows the learner to reflect on personal understandings. It is also good for the learners to review previous feedback from subordinates, peers, and bosses. This data can come from any source i.e. survey, performance review or casual conversation.

Climate

The concept of climate has not only physical application but it relates to setting an environment that is trust worthy, free of criticism and honest. The facilitator can establish a contractual commitment with the learners. The information shared is not to be repeated, distributed, or shared in any fashion beyond those walls. This provides the learners with the comfort of knowing that anything they share is respected and controlled. With this agreement, the session shows mutual respect for each learner in the environment. In the physical aspect, the facilitator responsibility is to make the room setting pleasurable and comfortable in all formats. The room appearance actually aids the learner in focused thinking.

Planning

The facilitator comes prepared for the class. This means any resource information, personal information, survey information and actual learning needs. The facilitator has detail curriculum specifically for this course. We do not want to waste time during the course developing the overall purpose of the course.

Diagnosis of Needs

As planning takes place, the facilitator should have analyzed data on learners. The facilitator's opportunity to understand the needs of the learners takes place during registration of the course. The facilitator's overarching purpose is identified during marketing and publicity of the course. The facilitator can review any personality data that maybe available. The facilitator can make assumptions from the data provided. The analysis of personality, background, and future goals gathered from this employee data assist in the flow development of the course.

Setting of Objectives

The facilitator shall have an overall purpose for the course. The purpose can be board initially. The facilitator should work with the learners to develop internal course objectives. The facilitator should stir the learners in the directions of needs listed by the facilitator and learners. This process builds commitment by the learners to obtain the objectives. The learner's movitation to achieve assist the facilitator in moving the class forward. The learner owns the objectives and is more incline to complete the work necessary to develop internally.

Designing Learning Plans

Preparation for the course requires that the facilitator take some time to understand the audience taking part in the course. The facilitator creates a strategy for completing the course based on the information received. Most settings provide the facilitator with information about the character of the learners. Observation details who the natural leaders of the group are and who are group participants. The facilitator organizes the course with that information defined. Defining the strategy using the Strengths, Weakness, Opportunities and Threats method allows the facilitator to have a counter action and even action for a class, in which the learners are described. The facilitator's communication method detail development in this process also. The facilitator considers role-play, open discussion, lecture, or games.

For example, in preparing the course for a group that has all first level managers a strength to consider is the education level and experience of the students. In many cases, the class will have an age gap; this can be considered a strength. These two strengths are areas in which the facilitator can move the students to build relationships. The learning is an opportunity. Threats may come from first level managers who have been in that role for five years or more.

The development of role-play and open discussion are important and address the over purpose for the course.

Learning Activities

The learning activity detail is the course curriculum. The course developed for this KAM provides leadership learners awareness of internal conflicts with corporate values and personal values.

The curriculum is as follows:

Proposed Teaching Title:

When did the WAR begin? A reflect view of corporation values and your personal core values.

Objective/Purpose of training

Purpose (Questions to be Answered):

- How do you live the company's values?
- Do we have internal conflicts with the corporate values?
- How should we respond to those conflicts?
- Can we agree with the goals and objectives of our leadership?

- Do these conflicts affect your management judgment?
- Does the conflict affect you home environment?
- How can we connect the two worlds?

Actions for the facilitator

1. Complete per-setup of seating chart.
2. Each day remove student's amenities. This is to evoke an emotional response.
    a. Day 1 all laptops and cell phones are to be removed.
    b. Day 2 Move seating arrangement and remove all except one writing pad. Student is not to have additional writing materials.
    c. Day 3 Move seating arrangement and leave one writing utinsel and two sheets of paper in the seating area. Please provide mapping sheets and action plan sheets.
    d. Day 4 Move seating arrangement and leave a box of caryons and one sheet of paper in the seating area.
3. Observe students reactions.

Illustration of good/bad performance

Introduction:

The world we live in requires us to be tolerant, kind, and forgiving. The question of where to apply such characteristics comes up frequently. Of course, we should be kind in every situation. We are asked by our company's to be loyal and trust the decisions of the leadership. Is that a smart move? There are requirements the dictate what we should do in all situations. More often than not, we agree with the position and movement of our bosses. Every company has a "Charter", Mission Statement" and "Customer Value" measure. Our goals and objectives align with those "Charters", "Mission Statements", and "Customer Values".

The purpose of this course is to assist first level manager in identifying, reflecting and addressing conflicts with their company's value system. Human behavior teaches us to avoid conflict. We are reminded that we are to be nice, kind and caring people. In the corporate environment situations occur where conflict is a requirement. Do we handle these situations very well? Are the actions required against the moral fiber of our being? The value system in which we developed is it correct. Does it take into account a variety of places and events?

In the process of living, the companies values are you ignoring your own values and the reverse can be true also. In the process of living, your values are you ignoring the company's values. What affect does that have on your work environment? What affect does that have on your home environment? Are your internal fears contributing to the actions you take?

The obvious question is what is a conflict. A conflict is a disagreement, a difference, or a contradiction between various items, thoughts, or people. It is identifies that there may be a problem or issue. When such things occur within human beings, there is a belief that there is a bad feeling that comes along with it. Whatever happens in your system it is something you want to avoid. (This is an area for discussion and debate for the learners. Develop real-time definitions and the physical response that develops during the conflict.)

The facilitator takes areas of the charter and makes them class learning activities. Example, Charter Statement = "To deliver quality"

I. Evaluation of the present
    a. How do you live the company's values?
        i. How are company's values communicated?
            1. Review the company's communication model
            2. Discuss methods to improve
            3. Presenting those methods and describe in as much detail as possible

ii. What is your company Charter or Mission Statement?
   1. Recite the Charter and Mission Statement without assistance
   2. Write it on the white boards
   3. Underline the important points of the Charter and Mission statement
   4. What is wrong with it: what is right with it?

Facilitator note and disagreements: Based on the process of Argyris (1983) evaluate areas where there is a focus of what wrong outside of the students. The learning is in being aware of self-motivations and internal responses.

iii. Is there an alignment between the Charter and Mission Statement?

This allows the learner to make external inferences, yet with true data.

iv. How do you align with those values?

This is another area of inference with a need to become more self-aware. By using Argyris' methods of double loop within this section, the facilitator can build the discussion platform.

Potential Discussion Question: *Develop a looping process with recorder to evaluate the data provided.*

b. Do we have internal conflicts with the corporate values?

The purpose of this section of question is to move the learner to reflection and discomfort. The learner's motivation and awareness of the impact on them personally is to discuss the undiscussable.

i. Are there values you do not agree with?
ii. What emotional impact if any does that involve?

       iii. How do we responds to the emotional discomfort?
       iv. Are we aware of how the discomfort may appear to subordinates?
  c. How should we respond to those conflicts?
       i. What is a good response to a bad situation?
       ii. What is our view of the people involved?

There is a certain level of inference made at this point about upper management and employees. The facilitator should re-direct the process for self-evaluation and observation.

       iii. Should we always focus on positive view of the actions?
  d. Can we agree with the goals and objectives of our leadership?
       i. Does your performance evaluation reflect what you want to be measured on?
       ii. Complete role-play sheet. (Broad all responses)
          1. What was the response?
          2. Takes notes real-time by boarding information.
          3. What are the questions; are they internal or external?
          4. Document any information that flows upward to the overall Charter and/or Mission statement.
          5. What are the inferences made by the role-play?
       iii. Was any information connected to real life experiences?
       iv. Return to acknowledgement of fears and lack of understanding.
  e. Does the conflict affect your home environment?
       i. What attributes of your corporate environment are rules in your home?
       ii. If not, do you think there should be?
       iii. How does your family feel about those rules?
  f. How can we connect the two worlds?

      i. Are the systems on different ends of the spectrum?
     ii. If so why, if not why not?
    iii. Is there anything of values in the charter that a family can apply?

II. Understanding the emotional make up of the learners
    a. Emotional Development (Broad the data received)
        i. With each review of the Charter and Mission statement what is the emotional response?
       ii. Are the learners concerned about the message communicated?
      iii. Should the emotional information be communicated down?
      iv. Male and female emotional processing

Conceptual Model

III. Connecting personal values to corporate values (Charter Statement = "To deliver quality.")
    a. Process in Action (develop a personal map)

Elements of the model

        i. Define the Charter Statement
       ii. Evaluation in detail what does that mean in your system development process.
           1. How is that statement accomplished? (what have you observed?)
           2. Is it ethical? (What does the culture expect?)
           3. Bring to the fore-front the conflicts? Discuss in detail.
           4. Understand that these are the learners premises i.e. truths.
      iii. Are there conflicts in the system process that need addressing?
           1. Behavioral strategies internally developed.

2. Are there Personal changes?
    a. Achieve the company's purpose?
    b. Win do not lose
    c. Suppress negative feelings
    d. What makes sense to do, rationally think it through?
3. Are there corporate changes?
    a. Achieve the company's purpose
    b. Win do not lose
    c. Suppress negative feelings
    d. What makes sense to do, rationally think it through?
  iv. Reflection of disconnects
  v. Bridging the gaps
    1. If this were a situation at home, how would you handle it?
  vi. Repeat on as many Charter statements as time will allow.

In this application, additional work sheets provide to assistance in the learning process. In the event the facilitator cannot provide those items, they are relatively easy to create. The facilitator should review the core values of the students. Argyris (2008) documents the four basic values of human behavior. The values are

- Remain in independent control
- Maintain a wining role and position also limit losing anything
- Smother negative feelings
- Maintain a rational perspective that would align to developed objectives

This area analysis allows the facilitator to increase the learning throughout the course process. These underline values exist in the individual's values documented during the course. The facilitator can investigate the layers that may exist in the implementation of this course. This is all because this course is specific to examine individual value systems.

Techniques and Practice/role playing

    b. If you are not a part of the solution then you are part of the problem. Be aware of the group's dynamics.
        i. Where do you step-up?
        ii. How do you response to the negative feelings?
        iii. Is truth a requirement?

Managerial implications discussion

IV. Evaluate the personal map created in Section III
    a. Moving the information to your personal work environment (Develop an Action Plan)
        i. Do you need to build personal relationships before delivering message?
            1. If yes, seek HR assistance to do this.
        ii. Determine a method of communication for personal connection (nothing electronic).
            1. One-on-one
            2. All-hands
        iii. Determine personal response to questions.
        iv. Is there still some internal conflict?
            1. Fear
            2. Dictate
            3. Honesty
        v. Develop a plan of action to deal with your internal conflicts
            1. Read
    b. Be aware of the reflection "Notice the board in your own eye"

V. The seating arrangement changes and the amenity changes
    a. The actions are noted to the facilitator in the beginning of the course.

  i. Day 1 has little to no emotional response.
  ii. Day 2 furstration begins because of the lack of utinsels.
    1. Note that this is all that provided
    2. Highlight the corporate conflict with meeting the needs of the employees
    3. Write them on White broad keep them posted.
  iii. Day 3 angry will appear and compromises on how to take notes
    1. Reasoning in the map and action plan development
    2. Bewilderment on why – reflect on the learners actions
  iv. Day 4
    1. Bewilderment on why – reflect on the learners actions
    2. Note the compromises in providing something else.
    3. Note the frustration
    4. Discuss the emotional re-actions

VI. Evaluate class and feedback from learners.
  a. Develop survey on white broad
    i. Ask the standard questions
      1. Course
        a. Did we achieve objectives
        b. Was the course though provoking?
        c. Was it an open environment?
        d. Is anything worth taking back to you job area?
      2. Physical Environment
      3. Facilitator Feedback
      4. Better next time
      5. Would you recommend the course

VII. Conclusion

The learners should have completed a personal map and created an action plan. The need is to move the process from thought to action. It is not to focus on the negative reasoning that may occur, but to develop a system of assistance. The desire of the facilitator is to facilitate action and responsibility. The learning developed assist in building commitment to the corporation. The learning developed assist in building commitment to self-truth and continued internal growth.

Evaluation

The evaluation of the course is a mutual process that allows the learners to communicate their thoughts and views. It allows the facilitator to receive feedback to better structure the course, if necessary. The evaluation process also allows the learners and the facilitator to assess the over need of the course. This is an important step in the process to measure the true learning of the students. The process shows a mutual level of respect and consideration for the other group.

The learner can use tools provided in this packages to document and compare their internal premises and their environments truths. The overall objective to the process is to develop an unbiased view of self and the organizations.

In summary, the expectation is that the facilitator has developed a system to understanding the needs of the class. The facilitator's verification of connections to personal experience and the present information are important. The learners' degree of discussion should detail the level of double loop learning. The course is structure for 8 hours for 5 days. This provides the facilitator with time to examine areas of need.

The applications of Argyris' methods have proven to be successful in organization environments. Even though Argyris' method applications are groups, it is applicable at an individual level. By integrating the looping in organizational training individuals are able to understand their theory-in-use.

Knowles' defined processes for adult course creation provided the backbone structure for this course. I wanted to combine the method to magnify the learning. The determination of the learner's fundamental premises is important in developing an action for results. The implementation of looping builds in the development of that knowledge specifically from the learners. The examination of the learner's premises in comparison to world truths builds on that learning. In this application it is important acknowledge the hard data and make alignments.

The looping process in the Whole and –Part-Whole structure gives the learner the opportunity to complete detail analysis of data. Looping develops connections to life experiences and the provided data by the individual. As stated be Argyris this process increases learning when the individual has the ability to reflect on internal behaviors.

Supplemental Package For the Implementation Of this Workshop

Role Play scripts:

Manager –to-Employee Conversation

(Hall-way conversation)

Character: Manager, employee

Manager: "Good Morning."

Employee: "Good Morning."

Manager: "We have a lot of good programs ahead of us."

Employee: sarcastically "Yes we do."

Manager: "These are exciting times."

Employee: sarcastically "Sure are."

Manager: "This is a great opportunity for us."

Employee: "Yeah." (employee walks away)

Peer-to-Peer Conversation

Character: Manager#1, Manager#2

Enter right side of coffee center.

Manager#1: "Good Morning."

Enter left side of coffee center.

Manager#2: "Good Morning."

Manager#1: "What did you think about that message yesterday given by the VP?"

Manager#2: "The VP said everything the press wanted him to say."

Manager#1: "Really, it all matched our Charter and Mission."

Manager#2: "Yeah but it stated that we are bending over backwards for our customer."

Manager#1: "That means extra work and hours."(sadness)

Manager#2: "But hopefully bigger bonuses."

Manager#1: "What is the price?"

Manager#2: "That's what you signed up for when you signed on the dotted line."

Manager#1: "Oh, well another day."

Value Mapping

Values to Compare	Corporate Value	Corporate Value	Corporate Value	Corporate Value	Corporate Value
Individual Value					
Individual Value					
Individual Value					
Individual Value					
Individual Value					
Individual Value					
Individual Value					
Individual Value					
Individual Value					
Individual Value					

References

Argyris, C. & Schon, D. (1974). Theory in Practice. San Francisco: Jossey-Bass.

Argyris, C. (1982). Reasoning, Learning and Action. Individual and Organizational. San Francisco: Jossey-Bass.

Argyris, C. (1923). Teaching Smart People How to Learn. Harvard Business School Publishing (2008) Boston, Massachusetts.

Atwater, J. B., Kannan, V. R., Stepehens, A. A. (2008). Cultivating system thinking in the next generation of business leaders. *Academy of Management Learning & Education*, 7, 1, 9-25.

Avolio, B.J., Hannah, S. T., (2008). Developing readiness: Accelerating leader development. *Consulting Psychology Journal: Practical and Research*, 60, 4, 331-3347.

Bolton, F.C. (2006). Rubrics and Adult Learners: Andragogy and Assessment. *Assessment Update*, 18, 3, 5-6.

Boyatzis, R.E., Saatcioglu, A. (2008). A 20-year view of trying to develop emotional, social and cognitive intelligence competencies in graduate management education. *Journal of Management Development*, 27, 1, 92-108.

Bryson, L. (1936). Adult Education. New York: American Book Co.

Bryson, L (1938). Administration of Adult Education. New York: American Book Company.

Chaffin, A. J., Harlow, S. D. (2005). Cognitive Learning Applied to Older Adult Learners and Technology. *Educational Gerontology*, 31, 4, 301-329.

Clarke, M., Bailey, C., Burr, J. (2008). Leadership development: making a difference in unfavorable circumstances. *Journal of Management Development*, 27, 8, 824-42.

Dallmer, D. (2004). Collaborative Test Taking With Adult Learners. *Adult Learners*, 15, 3/4, 4-7.

Forrest III, S. P., Peterson, T. (2006). It's Called Andragogy. *Academy of Management Learning & Education*, 5, 1, 113-122.

Hussein, J. W. (2008). An existential approach to engaging adult learners in the process of legitimizing and constructing meanings from their narrative knowledge. *Action Research*, 6, 4, 391-420.

Joo, K.H., Kim, S.H (2009), Development and Application of an Efficient Ubiquitous Teaching and Learning Model. *Advanced Communication Technology, 2009. ICACT 2009. 11th International Conference* Volume 03, 15-18 Feb. 2009 Page(s):2165 - 2168

Knowles, M. (1984). The Adult Learner: A Neglected Species (3rd Ed.). Houston, TX: Gulf Publishing.

Knowles, M. & Knowles, H. (1966). Introduction to Group Dynamics: New York, N.Y.: Associate Press.

Lamoureux, K. (2008). Developing Leaders. *Leadership Excellence*. 25, 7, 11-12.

Mccormick, I., Burch, G. St.J. (2008). Personality-focused coaching for leadership development. *Consulting Psychology Journal: Practice and Research*, 60, 3, 267-278.

Quick, J.C., Nelson, D.L. (2008). Leadership development: On the cutting edge. *Consulting Psychology Journal: Practice and Research*, 60, 4, 293-297.

Sticht, T.G. (1976). Comprehending reading at work. In M. Just & P. Carpenter (eds.), Cognitive Processes in Comprehension. Hillsdale, NJ: Erlbaum.

Tain, A. (2007). The Study of Distance Adult Training Mode Based on the Network Games. *Information Technologies and Applications in Education, 2007. ISITAE '07. First IEEE International Symposium* on 23-25 Nov. 2007 Page(s):494 – 497.

Taylor, K. (2006). Brain function and adult learning: Implications for practice. *New Directions for Adult & Continuing Education*, 110, 71-85.

Veith, C. S., Smith, T. W... (2008). Engineering and Technical Leadership Development: Challenges in a Rapidly Changing Global Market. *Chief Learning Officer*, 7, 2, 46-49.

Weick, C. W. (2008). Issues of consequence: Lessons for educating tomorrow's business leaders from philosopher William James. *Academy of Management Learning & Education*, 7, 1, 88-98.

Made in the USA
San Bernardino, CA
31 March 2014